A Pra
Run

MW01028363

Festina Lente

Peter Hoffmann partnered Steve Ovett and Sebastian Coe as one of Great Britain's three 800 metres athletes at the 1978 European Championships in Prague and was also part of the 1976 Olympic 4 x 400 metres squad at Montreal. Peter Hoffmann was educated at Hunters Tryst School Oxgangs Edinburgh and at Boroughmuir Senior Secondary School. After graduate and post-graduate studies in Edinburgh he worked for SCVS; the Scottish Episcopal Church; the private sector and thereafter mainly in local government as a chief officer in education; culture and sport. This book is part of the pentalogy of five athletics based books by the author which encapsulate the social culture of the Edinburgh era of the 1970s; - A Life In A Day In A Year: A Postcard From Meadowbank, 1973-1978 (2017); Festina Lente - A Practical Philosophy of 800 Metres Running (2018); The True Confessions Of Retep Nnamffoh: School's Out For Ever, A 1973 Edinburgh Young Athlete's Diary (2018);You Can Run But You Can't Outrun Yourself: A 1950s Edinburgh Love Story (2021) and Audacity and Idiocy – A Scottish Athlete's 1978 Commonwealth Games Journal (2022).Peter is available for athletics advice on 400 and 800 metres running and may be contacted at
peter.hoffmann@btinternet.com

Peter Hoffmann

A Practical 800 Metres Running Philosophy

Festina Lente

Excellent read! I agree wholeheartedly with everything you advocate. This needs to be out there for all aspirants to read.

Paul Forbes, 8 Nations 800 metres champion 1980

'This is "the bible" for two lap specialists and coaches who understand the truth that 800m is a sprint not an endurance event!'

Paul Baxter

'Loved reading this. A refreshing outlook on training for 800m in an era when we are bombarded with technical references to lactate threshholds, VO2 max, macro/meso/micro cycles etc. Keep it simple seems to be the ethos - but with a balanced approach to the hard work, speed work and conditioning required. Follow Peter's straightforward philosophy and you will have every chance of fulfilling your potential.'

Gregor Nicholson

Contents

Introduction

Afterword

A Hypothetical 800 metres Training Fortnight and a Summer Racing Schedule

Postscript 2021

Wish upon a star

'…Questions unanswered
Questions not asked
Some are worth knowing
Some left in the past
Go in with eyes open
Your life will be grand
Just give it your damndest
And go lead the band...'

Roger Turner

Peter Hoffmann chasing Seb Coe down the home straight in the 800 metres at the 1978 UK Championships, but alas, too late.

Introduction

Hold this thought in mind as you read this small monograph – to run a world class 800 metres requires only around one minute and forty-five seconds of hard effort and yet many aspiring athletes out there base some of their training on running 100 miles per week, relatively slowly.

Forty years ago back in 1978 I ran a half mile in 1 minute 46 seconds, still a respectable performance today. To put that run into context, at the time, Steve Ovett had only run a second quicker. Indeed, at that time my ambition was to have raced Coe and Ovett down the home straight in the race of the century at the 1980 Olympic Games 800 metres final in Moscow.

Most runners look back on their careers feeling they never quite fulfilled their potential. As the old saw goes *if* is the saddest word in the English language. *If only I had…* Like many of you out there, from a distance of forty years I discern many good patterns of what we did well but also some key mistakes too which of course tear at the soul. And talking of souls, Father Gianni in the recent BBC series set in Tuscany, Second Chance Summer, expressed it rather beautifully when he said: '*…the problem is you only learn with age and experience, so by the time you realise you have learnt a lot of things unfortunately a lot of time has passed and many chances have been lost.*'

But for others - today's and tomorrow's young athletes it is not too late. Ben Jones, M.D. said '*The saddest thing about dying is that all the stuff you've learned goes in to the ground with you. Make sure you pass it on before you croak.*' From a distance and following Ben's advice, here's my starter for ten - a palimpsest - 10 simple tips to run your optimum half mile by practicing the golden mean.

Unlike the book *A Life In A Day In A Year* which describes over 500 pages the day to day life, training and racing of a budding international half miler this small essay or monograph takes the opposite approach by distilling that experience and the knowledge gained into a succinct programme which cuts to the quick, outlining the key steps to follow to run a swift 800 metres.

But first, a health warning. I'm neither a coach; nor a sports scientist; nor an academic, but instead someone who has run for almost 60 years - a reflective practitioner. This is not an academic nor a scientific treatise which works back from the demands of the event relating them to your strengths and weaknesses and accordingly tailors a training programme based on lactate tolerance or VO2 levels, etc. Instead, it offers some practical, simple, common-sense tips garnered from a lifetime's experience of running from beginner, to international, to fun runner. I'm advocating a simple approach, but one which I sincerely believe will help any half miler run their best performance.

At the outset I want to make four key points. First, although I'm targeting this advice at international class athletes it's equally applicable to aspiring youngsters wishing to run a great half mile too or indeed any master's athlete out there - just apply the principles and alter the times.

Second, unlike say the great Arthur Lydiard I don't advocate undertaking separate programmes throughout the seasons of the year; instead I nail my colours to the mast and advocate one which has an ongoing circular approach with each small cycle feeding into the next one; thus the training should be broadly similar throughout the year with the only natural variances being that come the racing season, with the warmth from better weather and the motivation of racing and also the need to taper prior to certain key competitions, the quality will improve and the quantity of repetitions will be reduced.

Third, it's not rocket science.

A good analogy is with a car.

It needs a good engine; it should have a nice efficient line to it with an excellent power to weight ratio; it should also have that torque under the bonnet when you really need it; and finally it should have enough fuel to get you through your journey from A to Z without being too fancy. This will mean undertaking the appropriate sessions that will help develop muscle mitochondria, your ability to cope with lactic acid, etc.

And fourth and last, when you are constructing your training programme it is useful to have in mind how difficult or challenging or intense certain sessions are.

I use my own grading system of **(Ex)** Extreme; **(VH)** Very Hard; **(H)** Hard; **(A)** Average; and **(E)** Easy.

A good rule of thumb is at the very most to never undertake more than one Extreme; one Very Hard; and one Hard session in a 7 or 8 day cycle.

By the way, Extreme is pretty much eye-balls out! And close to race effort.

If you adopt this recommended approach to your training you'll fly a half mile.

Aged fifteen the beginning of the half mile dream - Paul Forbes (1:45) and Peter Hoffmann (1:46) Meadowbank Edinburgh 1972

Chapter 1

Dream, Baby; Dream

You need to have a dream to sustain you over the years; so, find what motivates you to get out there season in season out to train in all weathers and to push yourself in races when your body is screaming at you to stop.

In the 1920s the writer and mythologist Joseph Campbell (who also happened to be one of America's finest half milers) wrote of following your bliss:

If you do follow your bliss, you put yourself on a kind of track that has been there all the while waiting for you, and the life you ought to be living is the one you are living. When you can see that, you begin to meet people who are in the field of your bliss, and they open the doors to you. I say, follow your bliss and don't be afraid, and doors will open where you didn't know they were going to be. If you follow your bliss, doors will open for you that wouldn't have opened for anyone else.

Find your dream, then follow it; and remember - *Festina Lente* - Make haste, slowly.

Chapter 2

Control Your Weight

Ensure your weight is at its ideal level.

If it's not, you won't fulfil your potential. Simple fact.

But that doesn't mean being as light as possible. Too often I see good international runners who are actually too thin.

Don't sacrifice lightness for strength. Instead, what you're really after is the optimum power to weight ratio.

So, it's better to be two or three pounds heavier with good power than to be too light with little power. The best athletes often glide effortlessly over the track with controlled power. Think Ovett at his peak over 1500 metres at the 1977 World Cup.

1977 World Cup men's 1500 metres (Getty Images)

Control and monitor your weight; if you do need to lose anything, do so, but very, very slowly. Be patient. If you've gained some weight you will have done so over a period of time. To lose it, do so similarly. A pound a week is aplenty and you will hardly notice the effort; yet over 6 months that would add up to almost two stones!

Eat regular, balanced, healthy tiffins every few hours. For hard longer sessions you need a good store of carbohydrates in your system.

Whilst advocating a focus on a high carbohydrate, medium fat and protein diet, avoid sugar like the plague.

Drink plenty of water.

I would advocate a variable approach to your daily diet as determined by the demands of the day and the type of training sessions undertaken.

You need to think about 3 Ts - the *type* of fueling; the *timing* and also the *total* number of calories you are consuming.

On easy rest days this means something quite different to intensive sessions where it's important to up your protein uptake to around 2gs per kilogram in weight.

If you are aiming to reduce weight – body fat – in principle don't neglect protein and instead later on in the day reduce your carbohydrates. This will help ensure you are not getting rid of lean muscle.

Most people know what they should be doing. At the end

of the day retire to bed in the evening knowing that when you awake the following morning you will be very slightly lighter.

Breakfasts could be either a bowl of porridge and a sliced banana or a bowl of Greek full fat yoghurt and hazelnuts or blueberries; and afterwards a 3 egg, cheese, mushroom and ham omelette or cheddar cheese and grapes. Two or three coffees can help to aid and improve your sessions too, but I wouldn't advocate them on race day, as the excitement and adrenaline of racing more than prepares you.

For lunch a bowl of home-made vegetable soup with a sandwich and some fruit is excellent; as is a very simple dish which takes 5 minutes in the microwave - salmon, peppers, tomatoes and mushrooms with a little brown rice cooked in soya and chilli sauce. Snack on almonds and fruit. And if you do need that treat, a square of 85% dark chocolate with a handful of hazelnuts should do the trick.

For your evening meal always include a decent carbohydrate alongside greens and your chicken or meat, only reducing the carbos if you're aiming to gradually reduce weight.

.

If you're approaching a race I would advise introducing carbohydrates at each tiffin and meal in the few days leading up to the race; and by then, you'll hopefully be at your aimed for race weight.

Peter Hoffmann winning 200 metres Pye Cup 1976 (John Scott)

Chapter 3

Practice Running FAST!

Speed is your greatest asset and by running fast I mean sprinting flat out several times each week.

Be honest with yourself - when did you last sprint as fast as you could putting the pedal flat to the floor? For most athletes it will be months - for others, years!

Unless you're a 60 metres indoors specialist or a 100 metres sprinter 99% of runners never practice running flat out so how can you expect to suddenly turn on the turbo-jets come a race especially if it's a year on from the previous summer!

A good approach is to incorporate the all-important strength sessions after your 30-50 metres sprints; do this several times each week e.g. 8 x 30 metres with a good recovery walking 370 metres between each sprint.

And that's just to maintain your speed. By the time you get into your early 20s your performance will deteriorate.

Incorporating pure sprints into your training programme will help make the key middle distance sessions easier and swifter too. In your warm up incorporate 6 x 30 metre technique sprints getting quicker and quicker with each one.

In Scotland in particular but in Britain generally it's difficult to practice running fast throughout the year; so, when you're young and free find a way to escape abroad for up to three months when the weather is at its worst.

Chapter 4

Strength and Power

But better still, rather than just maintaining speed let's improve it by improving your power. Research shows that by getting into the gym or similar two or better still three times each week will do this and improve your running performance; do weights and gym work and incorporate some speed drills and a few plyometrics into your warm-up before you start your track sessions.

The focus should be on your legs and less so on your arms. However, it's very helpful to work on and practice your arm action in front of a mirror aiming for 400 or 800 metres efforts timewise. Do this using some hand weights – up to 2lb in weight, preferably lighter.

In the off season run fast 20 second hill repetitions up a slight incline wearing a weights jacket - they're great for developing your quads.

Do a Togher general body weight circuit which includes lots of stepups, bench jumps, bench jumps astride and aside and core-work (sit-ups and planks) – if you think about it everything comes from the core – your arms and your legs, so it's imperative that you're in good nick there; or and indeed alternatively get along to a Metafit session which is also a valuable cardio workout too. Work your glutes. Do squats. Do step-ups. Do one leg squats wearing a weights jacket.

Often these can follow a short sprints session. As a rule of thumb some experts recommend that to build muscle size your sessions should aim for 3 sets 10 reps at 70% percent of your one-rep best; to build strength aim for 3 sets of 6 reps at around 85% of your best; and to develop power 3 sets 8 reps at 50% of your max.

And after the session ensure you eat soon after the workout – around 25 grams of protein e.g. a tuna sandwich; a glass of milk; and a handful of hazelnuts or almonds.

On those days when you're not doing a full weights or strength workout, after your earlier running session finish the day by doing a short sharp mini-workout at home or in the yard incorporating a non-stop 5-10 minute leg session of e.g. 10 rear lunges; 10 Bulgarian split squats (leg on a bench); 10 Romanian deadlifts; 50 squats and 50 each leg single leg step-ups and 15 jump leg tucks finishing off with 50 cross sit-ups. Complete this workout with 1-2 lb barbells and practice 300 fast arm action in front of the mirror to complete the mini-workout – it should take you less than ten minutes.

When you feel the impact it has on your legs and how well it transfers to your running you'll wonder why it took you years to discover this.

But, on top of that, here's something very different.

Many athletes' performances tail off towards the end of the season. Commentators say this is due to tiredness or getting stale and lacking motivation. I believe it's more to do with the fact that after the spring most athletes neglect strength-work through the summer months.

So here's a radical proposal – forget about any steady running outwith warming up and warming down – steady running will do nothing for your performance: over the summer racing season simply alternate track sessions and weights/gym/resistance sessions. Maintain a light snappy strength-work programme throughout the summer track season. The track sessions themselves should alternate between a quarter miler's session and an 800 metre session. Thus Resistance/400m/Resistance/800m/Resistance...

In 1984 Coe was still in the gym a week before the Los Angeles Olympics.

Similarly, Salazar likes to see Farah et al keep that snap going throughout the racing season.

You won't need to do so many repetitions - just do enough to maintain your power to weight ratio from the spring throughout the summer months; and perhaps ease off altogether ten days before your main competition of the season.

Your ultimate goal is to reach the stage that when you're running fast at race pace that your legs are so strong that you just glide effortlessly over the track with a relaxed arm carriage for balance knowing there is a further gear there.

When you reach this point in your career it's the most wonderful feeling and will inspire greater confidence in what you might yet become.

Chapter 5

Cardiovascular System

To run a good half mile you need a reasonable aerobic base; equally importantly you need to be fit enough to undertake the key middle distance track sessions.

The best way to do this is through long slow easy steady running at conversation pace which will improve capillary development; increase the myoglobin content of your muscle fibres; and also mitochondria development.

I recommend doing such a steady run of around 40 minutes to an hour each week. But you will end up supplementing this when you warm up and warm down for 10-15 minutes for your track and gym sessions on other days adding another 20-30 minutes of daily aerobic running – aim to always do at least a 10 - 20 minute warm down jog.

In the off-season every couple of weeks incorporate into your schedule an easy long, steady run of up to 90 minutes.

If a 5k Parkrun happens to fall on such a day give it a go - it will give you a useful base line as well as motivating you to run fast and hard on occasion.

But quality and speed and tiredness should never be sacrificed at the altar of high mileage. There's a trade-off and that needs to be in favour of track work and the gym.

If high mileage was the key to running fast half miles then all those millions of runners churning out 70 mpw would be running them. Generally, they don't. And when they do it's the exception that proves the rule.

Chapter 6

Box Clever

There are lots of little maxims out there; some of them are wise.

Amongst them, less is more, is excellent advice.

The Greeks had a word for it - practice the golden mean - nothing in excess, everything in moderation.

Most often you should only train once a day and rest up for 24 hours before your next session.

It will help prevent injuries in the long term; help you recover from the previous day; and equally importantly you'll have a zest for the next session.

Similarly, it's better to under-train than to over train.

As mentioned, escape abroad to the warmth when the weather is at its worst.

The only occasion to do a double session is to incorporate a further weights/gym-work session into your week; the best day to do this is when you're undertaking your easy run.

Try to always run with the wind - practice running quickly and with good technique. And talking technique, if you don't have it, identify with someone who does and copy them.

El Guerrouj was the most beautiful runner; as is Bernard Lagat.

Bernard Lagat and Hicham El Guerrouj (Getty Images)

It's still useful to have heroes; adopt a phenomenological approach; identify with someone you admire and respect and when those key moments of choice come along ask yourself how they might behave or react in this situation.

What would they do?

Closer to home find a good mentor.

When my good friend Paul Forbes (a 1 minute 45 seconds half miler) and I were teenagers we trained regularly with sub 4 minute miler Adrian Weatherhead.

He was a decade older and taught us much, mainly

informally often when we were warming up or warming down after a session or out in parkland doing a steady run.

Sub 4 minute miler Adrian Weatherhead and Paul Forbes (Bill Blair)

Get into a good training environment and squad.

Training should be hard, but fun.

Try to run sessions where sometimes you're the top dog - it's good to be confident and to reinforce this attribute; on other occasions run with peers to introduce a little bit of competition and edge; and occasionally train with people who are better than you, but not too often as you want to be a very positive athlete and racer. But such sessions will help push you and take you out of your comfort zone.

Paul Forbes and Peter Hoffmann training at Meadowbank, winter 1978 (John Scott)

Back in the 1970s, overseen by Bill Walker, at weekends we had the best training squad in the world featuring World 400 metres number 1 David Jenkins; World Student Games 400 metres silver medallist, Roger Jenkins; 8 Nations 800 metres gold medallist, Paul Forbes; GB 400 metres hurdle international, Norman Gregor; sub 4 minute miler, Adrian Weatherhead; as well as myself, an Olympian and European Junior silver medallist.

It meant that if we were running 6 x 500 metres each athlete would take one run from the front with Adrian on the last rep. It meant for a much higher quality session than we could have managed alone. But, it was also important to get away from that elite squad at other times to prevent burning ourselves out.

British 400m hurdles international Norman Gregor

Listen to your body.

What is it telling you?

Athletes tread a fine line - it's like being a tightrope walker making continuous fine adjustments to achieve that elusive balance between two polarities - being honest with yourself and staying disciplined - getting out there and just doing it, but also being sensible and taking the occasional day off too when you're feeling exhausted or coming down with a cold.; as mentioned above it's always better to under train than to over train.

And as in all important areas of life, prioritise.

You only have so much energy and those aspects of training that are most important should never be at the mercy of those areas which are less so.

Distribute your energy like it's gold and allocate it wisely.

Be at your freshest and at your very best for the key middle distance track sessions of the week.

Make sure you're turning up for these sessions with an eagerness - with an appetite - you're excited and slightly nervous and apprehensive and not knackered, tired or unenthusiastic, where you end up just going through the motions.

In other words don't sacrifice quality for quantity.

And talking of quality here's some further radical advice - simulate half mile racing - regularly.

Chapter 7

Simulate 800 metres running - regularly

Point **6.** above begged the question what do I mean by quality?

By quality I mean training at faster than your race pace.

It means races will then be partly run within your comfort zone.

Similar to athletes ignoring sprinting flat out throughout the year most half milers only ever run occasional flat out 600s; perhaps on fewer occasions than on the fingers of one hand, usually in the late spring.

And yet this is what they're expecting their bodies to do come a race! It's crazy.

So, get your body used to doing what it's expected to do come race time. Surely it's common-sense to practise this key aspect much much more regularly so that not only do you get used to running like this, but so that you become better too.

Each new season you hope to improve on what you've run the season before yet you've spent up to a year avoiding doing so!

So, here's a radical proposal - if you really want to run a fast half mile in 1.44 or better start running very fast 600 metres or similar every seven to ten days throughout the whole year.

Ideally you should be aiming to run them in 75 seconds or better. Otherwise how can you expect to turn up for an international meet 800 metres and run relaxed through 600 metres in 78 seconds and maintain that pace if you haven't been practicing it throughout the year; get your body accustomed to how it feels allowing it to make the key physiological adaptations.

Make it as easy as possible by using pacers and aim to run two or three in training at around 75 seconds with a full recovery; because of the adrenaline come race day you're more likely to be able to flow through the 600 metres mark in 78 seconds with a speed reserve for the last quarter of the race.

Looking back I regret not incorporating such a regime into our training slightly more often; the nearest Paul Forbes and I got was one lovely Sunday morning in May 1978 at Meadowbank running a relaxed session of 79; 78 and 77 seconds.

We should have done that session much more often.

More recently the controversial Taoufik Makhloufli ran an 800 metres in 1:44.5 (10 minutes recovery) followed by 500 metres in 65 seconds; 400 metres in 52 seconds and a 300 metres in 39 seconds, the last three runs with a four minute recovery.

An alternative good session which we did however use to do was to run a 600 metres (78 seconds); 500 metres (63 secs); 400 metres (48 secs); 300 metres (34 secs); and a 200 metres (22 secs) with a good recovery. Alternatively a 500 metres; 400 metres; 300 metres; and a 200 metres with a 3 minute recovery at quicker than race pace is excellent too.

Whatever you do, don't shy away from these sessions.

A further great session is 3 x 2 x 300 metres with a jog 100 metres recovery and full recoveries between sets.

Aim to run the first repetition in each set at 36 seconds.

Similarly, an incredibly tough session is 5 x 300 metres with a walk 100 metre recovery kicking off the first few repetitions in 37 seconds and thereafter holding on!

The world record holder David Rudisha liked to run a 400m/200m/400m/200m at his 800m goal pace with a 3 minute recovery. So if you're aiming to run 1:44 then your aim should be 52/26/52/26 seconds.

Nick Symmonds (a 1:42.9 performer) similarly liked to replicate half mile pace in training and sometimes ran 5 x 200 metres with a 2 minute recovery (25-26 seconds) followed by 4 minutes rest; then 2 x 300 metres (37-38 seconds) again with a 2 minute recovery but this time followed by 5 minute rest before completing the session with a quarter mile at maximum effort in around 52 seconds. He also advocates 3 x 400 metres (4 minute recovery) at quicker than race pace.

By incorporating these sessions and this regime into your training programme you will steal a march on your rivals.

Chapter 8

Bread and Butter Middle Distance Sessions

To run a great half mile you also need to run bread and butter middle distance sessions too.

In the off-season there's no harm in occasionally joining the milers for one of the more traditional middle distance sessions - 8 x 400s (1 minute recovery) or 4 x 600s (4 minutes rest) but they should be just that - occasional.

8 x 300 metres with a 3 minutes recovery starting with 37/38 seconds trying to hold that pace for as long as possible is excellent; and as mentioned under point **7.** run 5 x 300 metres with a rolling start with less than a one minute walk 100 metres recovery kicking off at 36/37 seconds before you tail off; this is very hard – a killer session indeed - in fact, label it **(Ex)** Extreme!

5 x 500 metres in 65 seconds with around a 5 minute recovery is good as is 2 x 4 x 200 metres (30 seconds recovery) at 24 seconds pace.

Clocks too are excellent for gradually bringing on a jaded tiredness as you try to maintain speed endurance and quality - 100-150-100 and 150-200-150 clocks (up and down in 10 metres) with a jog back 90 seconds recovery are excellent - they're niggly little sessions.

Chapter 9

Quarter Miling

To run a fast half mile you will need to be able to run a great quarter too.

Most half-milers neglect this area.

Peter Hoffmann 4 x 400 metres relay Meadowbank 1976

Sometimes I ask good half-milers what they can run for 400 metres; they will reply vaguely '*Oh! I've run sub 48 seconds.*'

But when you ask what they can run right here, right now there's a world of difference.

So, don't kid yourself.

Recently Elliot Giles ran a training session reeling off 3 x 400s with a 10 minute recovery in 48.8, 48.1 and 47.6.

To run fast over a quarter you need to incorporate regular quarter-mile sessions e.g. 3 x 300 metres flat out in around 34 seconds with a full recovery. Or a 100 metres; 200 metres; 300 metres; 200 metres; and a 100 metres with between 5 and 15 minutes recovery all at quicker than 400 metres race pace.

Like fast 600s aim to do this session once every ten days or so. You'll really feel the benefit.

Or, 8 x 100 metres with an easy 5-8 minutes' walk around the track recovery; you need that recovery to maintain the quality; it's a surprisingly tough little session.

4 sets of 6 back to back 50s with short recoveries (20-30 seconds and 4 minutes between sets) are great and not just for 400 meter running but for the half mile too. Not only do you run with speed and with rhythm developing your speed endurance but they really raise your heart-rate surprisingly high too. Incorporate this session every ten days or so.

And if you can, try and get regular slots in 4 x 400 metre relay teams – great for your running but also great fun too; and because it's from a rolling start it relates well to half miling.

Chapter 10

Three Rs - Resilience; Rest and Racing

David Moorcroft

Training and competition requires resilience.

A few people have this quality in spades – an inherent rod of steel running through them.

I've trained with former world 5000 metres record-holder David Moorcroft and regularly with Adrian Weatherhead too; with both of these athletes it was something inherent.

I've seen it too with many of the distance runners - the iron men of the iron ground who churn up the laps in cross country running. But the rest of us aren't quite so hardy.

However, you can help to overcome this with some clever stratagems.

Albert Camus wrote: *'In the depth of winter, I finally learned that within me lay an invincible summer.'*

Remember that dream.

Use it to motivate yourself.

Ask yourself what your success would mean to others who help you - your family, your friends as well as to you, yourself.

Develop mantras for when the going gets hard - *First to the tape First to the tape* or *Never give in Never give in.*
As usual, Kipling is good:

If

'…If you can fill the unforgiving minute
With sixty seconds' worth of distance run,
Yours is the Earth and everything that's in it,
And—which is more—you'll be a Man, my son…

If you can force your heart and nerve and sinew
To serve your turn long after they are gone,
And so hold on when there is nothing in you
Except the Will which says to them: "Hold on!"

If you're doing a hard reps session don't think too far ahead; leave thinking about the next run until towards the end of the recovery period; often people throw in the towel far too early.

Take one run at a time.

In the tough later reps of a session don't throw in the towel immediately.

Come the last burning rep simply take 50 metres at a time. *'I can only drop out at a 50 metres mark'.* Sometimes that 50 metres can stretch and extend to the whole 300 or 600 metres!

And when it becomes painful either embrace the pain - associate with it or alternatively disassociate from it, by deploying some distraction techniques.

David Hemery winning 1968 Olympic Games 400m hurdles

Some of you will recall the great BBC athletics commentator for forty years, David Coleman, and how he brought to life David Hemery's stunning Olympic run in Mexico, 1968 or Ian Stewart's magnificent 5000 metres win at the 1970 Commonwealth Games.

On occasion, when I struggled through a tough training session wanting to give up, come these last few repetitions, in my imagination I could *hear* Coleman's voice in my mind's-eye *'...and it's Hemery (Hoffmann) gambling on everything...he's really flying down the back straight...Hemery (Hoffmann) leads...it's Hemery (Hoffmann) Great Britain...it's Hemery (Hoffmann) Great Britain...and Hemery (Hoffmann) takes the gold...he killed the rest...he paralysed them...Hemery (Hoffmann) won that from start to finish...'*

And before I knew it the session was over and I'd run as best as I could and got through another tough work-out.

I guess it's called motivation - self-motivation.

Find it where you can.

And as the season approaches, your motivation will increase and you'll be able to push the barriers even further.

As for racing, Ecclesiastes 9:11 says '...*I returned, and saw under the sun, that the race is not to the swift, nor the battle to the strong, neither yet bread to the wise, nor yet riches to men of understanding, nor yet favour to men of skill; but time and chance happeneth to them all...*' so grab the opportunity in any race - be brave - show some chutzpah and seize the day;

sometimes a smarter more confident athlete can beat a better one - Matt Centrowitz ran a great race at the Rio Olympics in the 1500 metres.

Races are nerve-wracking so get used to handling them well by racing often - race under distance events such as 400 metres where there is slightly less pressure.

In the lead up towards your main goal of the season you will probably need to race around three half mile races beforehand; running the full distance helps adapt your body for that main effort; out-with that, prior to your early races a 90 seconds effort in training can be useful; for this effort get paced throughout with someone taking you through the quarter in around 50 seconds. You'll blow up, but you will get a great training effect which will bring you on.

Rest up before you race making sure you taper your training. The people who knew best how to bring athletes to their peak were the old Pro schools in Scotland training athletes for the famous century old Powderhall Sprint. Money talks. And some of those schools stood to make significant monies from the bookies.

In following a tiered system which incorporates 100 to miler sessions on alternate days and only training once a day means that you will only need occasional days off.

It's almost self-regulating as you'll do running sessions on 6 days out of 8 with t'other 2 days devoted to strength and power work; and of course by also doing 100 and 200 metre track sessions these will be less intensive than the specific middle distance sessions meaning that when you do tackle these efforts you will be relatively fresh bringing speed and power to each workout.

But the key here is to always listen closely to your body. And to be honest with yourself too. When you do feel below par, not looking forward to training, dragging your body around feeling stiff, sore and tired, then this is the time to take a day off – the day when you've lost your edge – lost your bite - and you're less than eager to train that day.

As you become more experienced you will recognise the signs – your heart rate may be a little higher or you're spending much of the day on the sofa feeling listless and not quite 100%.

Peter Hoffmann winning European Junior 400 metres semi-final Athens 1975

The third R is for racing.

Come the race, if you can and have the confidence to do so, aim to distribute your energy wisely in half-mile races - if you look at the 200 metre splits in races they are often very disproportionate and wasteful.

Aim to run the shortest distance and run even pace.

And if the pace is suicidal if you can run the first three bends in lane one at the back of the field and gradually make your effort down the back straight when others who have been injudicious fighting over early position begin to flag and tire. It's easier to pass them there and move into position come the final bend.

My final thought on racing is to ensure you're thoroughly warmed up having blown the 'carbon' out of the engine!

Too many athletes don't warm up sufficiently; and when the race kicks off it (naturally) comes as quite a shock to the system and can negatively impact mentally on their confidence too.

The older you are the more important this becomes.

How often have you found in training that it's the second or third repetition that's the easiest?

The first few runs feel hard because of the systemic shock; the later runs are hard because you're beginning to tire.

Whereas, on the intermediate repetitions you glide along, often effortlessly because your body is completely warmed up; make sure you go to the start line for races having struck the optimal balance so that you're ready to race from the bang of the gun.

Whether you're an international athlete, an aspiring one, or a master runner, adopt the above and you'll fly a half mile.

Good luck with your adventures and seize the day, because each summer you may only have a handful left when the stars in the heavens are so aligned.

As Socrates said *'Enjoy yourself, it's later than you think!'*

Afterword

A Hypothetical 800 metres Training Fortnight and a Summer Racing Schedule

By way of an afterword I detail below a suggested training fortnight followed by a radical tweak for the summer's racing period. In constructing a training programme over the period of a 'fortnight' – twelve days – I would recommend structuring it around five tiers or types of track sessions but undertaking six as you should aim to do a half mile session each 'week' i.e. every six days.

Therefore the five-pronged training approach is based on undertaking a 100 meter sprinter session; a 200 metre sprinter session; a quarter-miler workout; one that is purely half mile based; and the fifth and last such session which is miler based.

This means track based sessions either three or four times a week. That suited the likes of my good friend Paul Forbes and myself throughout our careers and we remained relatively injury free. However, if you're able to run on a good grass surface I would recommend mixing it up with sessions on an all-weather tartan track.

However this approach may not suit everyone depending on your particular constitution or as you get older. This takes you back to one of my earlier maxims about boxing clever.

But a good rule of thumb is to alternate a track day with either a 40-60 minute steady run or up to an hour's weights, plyometrics and gym work, thus over an eight day period you would undertake four track sessions, two decent runs and two intensive power resistance based sessions.

If you're older and find that ratio beyond you then a different good rule of thumb would be to alternate over each three day period with a very high quality track session on day one; on day two undertake between 30 and 60 minutes of weights; box jumps; plyometrics and gymwork; and on day three do either a steady run of between 40 minutes and an hour or after a warm up, run between 3k and 5k hard.

Tackle it it in that order to allow your tendons and muscles to recover from the speed and power sessions before you begin the cycle again.

As can also be gleaned by what's gone before I'm not persuaded by the argument that as you get fitter and fitter and better and better that you increase the quantity of repetitions nor the number of training sessions each week: instead you should work on improving the quality of each session as a way of ensuring you are are constantly progressing.

A Hypothetical 800 metres Training Fortnight

Day 1 (VH) 800 metre session 2/3 x 600 metres flat out (15-20 minute recovery)

Day 2 (E) Resistance session Weights; box jumps; plyometrics and gymwork with the focus on legs

Day 3 100 metre session 2 x 4 x 30 metres (3 minute recovery) (15 minute rest between sets) followed by speed drills (10 rear lunges; 10 Bulgarian split squats (leg on a bench); 10 Romanian deadlifts; 50 squats and 50 each leg single leg step-ups and 15 jump leg tucks finishing off with 50 cross sit-ups. Complete this workout with 1-2 lb barbells and practice 300 fast arm action in front of the mirror to complete the mini-workout – it should take you around ten minutes.)

Day 4 (H) 5k run at a good pace

Day 5 400 metre session (H) 100; 200; 300; 200; 100 (5-12 minute recovery) all runs at quicker than 400 metre race pace

Day 6 (E) Weights; box jumps; plyometrics and gymwork with the focus on legs

Day 7 (VH) 800 metre session 3 x 2 x 300 metres in 36 seconds with a jog 100 metres recovery; full rest between sets or 5 x 300 metres (walk/jog 100 metres recovery) 37-38 secs

Day 8 (E) 40-60 minute easy run followed by speed drills (10 rear lunges; 10 Bulgarian split squats (leg on a bench); 10 Romanian deadlifts; 50 squats and 50 each leg single leg step-ups and 15 jump leg tucks finishing off with 50 cross sit-ups. Complete this workout with 1-2 lb barbells and practice 300 fast arm action in front of the mirror to complete the mini-workout – it should take you around ten minutes.)

Day 9 200 metre session 5 x 150 metres (6-10 minute recovery) at 200 metre race pace or quicker

Day 10 (E) Weights; box jumps; plyometrics and gymwork with the focus on legs

Day 11 Miler session (H) 8 x 300 (3 minute recovery) at 800 metre pace

Day 12 (E) 40-60 minute easy run

A Hypothetical 800 metres Summer Racing Schedule

When it comes to the summer I want to recommend something quite radical. Other than around 10/15 minute warm up jogs and warm downs I would drop all steady running – quite simply it's not going to do anything for you. And instead focus on high quality speed-work and strength-work: in particular by continuing to do the latter you can gain an advantage over your peers who will have mostly neglected this area as the spring progresses through into the summer. Thus, I would suggest alternating one day with a resistance session in the gym with a track session. The track sessions should be taken from either a quarter miler's work-out or a half miler's.

Thus following this pattern: 400m/Resistance/800m/Resistance/400m…

The quarter-miler's sessions could be: 300m; 200m; 100m with full recoveries or 2 x 3 x 200m with a 3 minute recovery and a full recovery between sets.

For a half-miler session it could be a flat out 650m followed by 3 x 300m (1 minute rest in between); 4 x 200m (20 second recovery); and 6 x 100m turnarounds. You should take a full recovery between each batch. Another excellent 800m session is 2 x 3 x 300m with a walk 100m recovery at quicker than race pace with a full recovery between sets.

Postscript

As a reflective practitioner I find my thoughts continue to evolve particularly around three aspects – (i) that *less really is more* including helping to prevent injury, leading to more consistent medium to long term training on an ongoing basis and facilitating a focus on high quality workouts and sessions – (ii) the crucial importance of working on strength and power – and (iii) the unnecessity for doing much in the way of aerobic running.

Athletes and readers of this monograph should be similarly reflective and adjust their approach slightly and accordingly tweaking their schedule around the principles that I've promulgated.

Because you are taking 24 hours rest between sessions fewer rest days will be required. These should thus be taken when you're feeling tired and uninspired.

And one final tip – try to go for a 30 minute afternoon or evening walk at the end of the training day – you'll find it helps you tackle the following day's session.

Festina Lente! – make haste (my friend), (but) slowly.

Made in the USA
Middletown, DE
18 December 2022

19260340R00029